ALL THAT TRASH

The Story of the 1987 Garbage Barge

and Our Problem with Stuff

By Meghan McCarthy

A Paula Wiseman Book
Simon & Schuster Books for Young Readers
New York London Toronto Sydney New Delhi

The year was 1987, known for

a speedy white car . . .

boxy-looking computers . . .

big hair . . .

and a news story about tons of trash that wouldn't go away. The grand adventure began with an idea by Lowell Harrelson. He got word that a New York landfill was almost out of room. Harrelson had a solution. He would take New York's trash far, far away and solve all its garbage problems.

Lowell Harrelson, owner of National Waste Contractors in Alabama

Harrelson agreed to take 3,186 tons of trash from New York's almost full landfill in Islip. The trash at this landfill came from New York City and Long Island.

First, he rented a barge to carry the garbage.

Mobro 4000

Second, he got a tugboat and crew to tow the barge.

Break of Dawn

Captain Duffy St. Pierre

First Mate David Soto

Third, he found a place to dump it.

Welcome
TO
NORTH CAROLINA

STATE LINE

UNION COUNTY

Harrelson's plan was revolutionary: to let the steaming, oozing heap of garbage decompose, thus creating methane gas – and then energy!

The methane gas is captured in underground wells. A vacuum pulls the gas through a pipe system.

The collected gas is burned, which powers a generator where mechanical energy turns into electrical energy.

Then the electricity travels to a transformer, where it is changed from high-voltage electricity to lower-voltage electricity.

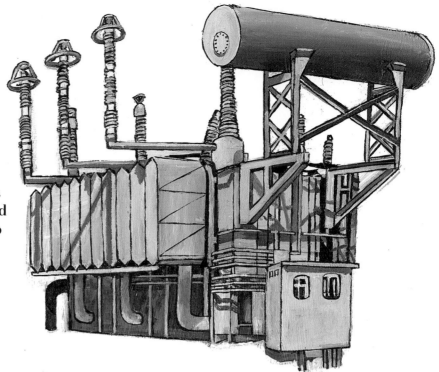

At last the electricity goes to power lines and then to your home!

As soon as the barge docked in North Carolina, the trouble began. A local reporter, looking for a good story, flew over the barge. On the six o'clock news that evening, the barge's presence was announced. Thanks to the report, an environmental official went snooping. That's when he observed medical waste on the barge.

Horrified, North Carolina officials obtained a court order, declaring that the garbage could not be dumped in their state.

Off went the *Break of Dawn*, apparently on its way to Alabama. Harrelson received a warning by phone indicating that Alabama didn't have room for his trash. Workers at the state docks were told to keep a lookout. It was clear that the garbage was *not* welcome in Alabama.

Next, the barge moved on toward Mississippi. The garbage, however, was not welcome there either, so it floated over to Louisiana. Louisiana thought it was so important that Harrelson not leave his garbage in their state that they hand-delivered him a letter.

The letter stated that Harrelson could not unload his garbage in the state of Louisiana. Obviously, the garbage was *not* welcome there.

A local port authority sent a boat out to guard the barge and tugboat. "I think what they [port authority officials] were worried about at first was that maybe the boat [towing the barge] might take off and leave the barge here," said a spokesperson.

By now the barge was infested with flies. Black ooze dripped from its bales.

The garbage barge was to remain at the mouth of the Mississippi until a solution could be found. When night fell, the patrol boat took a break from guard duty. That's when the *Break of Dawn* and the garbage barge disappeared! "What we're trying to find out now is if anybody knows just where it went to," said a Louisiana state official. Reporters tried to get Harrelson on the phone. His wife said that he was "out of town."

Where was the barge?

Finally, the barge was spotted floating in circles in the Gulf of Mexico. The mayor of Grand Isle in Louisiana said, probably with some relief, "Wherever this stuff goes, it's going to be somebody else's problem."

And it was.

The barge moved farther south until it arrived in Mexican waters. Being both offended and disgusted, Mexico reminded the United States of an agreement between the two countries banning the movement of toxic waste. "They are turning us into their very own garbage dump," wrote a Mexican newspaper.

For good measure, Mexico sent out its navy—four ships, two planes, and a helicopter.

The garbage was *not* welcome in Mexico. Where would it go? Some people thought it might go back to New York. But instead . . .

. . . it stopped in Belize, which is a small country in Central America. A spokesman for the government said, "The idea of us buying that garbage is laughable."

The country's defense force was swiftly sent to keep a lookout for the unwanted trash. *Nobody* wanted it.

That is, until a business owner in possession of a tiny island in the Bahamas called Little San Salvador had an idea. Papers wrote that he wanted to use the garbage to build up the island, and then plop his resort on top. The business owner said it was going to be "a fantastically beautiful island that everyone will want to see."

Or . . .

not. The Bahamian government did not like this idea one bit. It also sent out its defense force. The barge moved on. Where would it go next?

Days later, the *Break of Dawn* was spotted towing the garbage to the Florida Keys. Residents of the Keys were alarmed! They feared that the garbage would pollute their sunny beaches . . .

and ruin their colorful coral reefs.

Florida citizens wanted nothing to do with all that trash.

Federal environmental agents investigated. They zipped up white protective suits and snapped on protective breathing masks. They picked through the contents, looking for hazardous material. The *Break of Dawn*'s first mate called the suits "ridiculous." He added, "It's just ordinary garbage."

Reporters observed the following items:

magazines

clothing

old tires

cardboard

vacuum cleaner hose

carpet

By now the barge had received a lot of attention. Television anchors had plenty to say.

Finally, after almost two months, it appeared that there was a solution! The Islip town supervisor announced, "We're probably going to put some yellow ribbons outside the gates of the landfill to welcome our garbage back." And with that, the garbage began making its journey back to New York, back to where it came from. The plan was to dock the garbage in Queens, New York, and then drive it by truck to Islip.

But as the barge made its way to New York, it looked as though the plans were once again spoiled.

I don't want it squatting here.

NYC Deputy Mayor

We don't know what's in it. It's been sitting in the hot sun for weeks. It probably contains tropical insects and vermin.

Queens Borough President

A court hearing was scheduled in Queens. It was then that a judge approved a temporary restraining order, preventing those massive piles of trash from driving through Queens.

While in limbo, the barge docked in Brooklyn. There, city health inspectors climbed aboard and took their own samples for testing.

It's crazy, isn't it, to go through all of this just to return it to the people we took it from.

Duffy St. Pierre

We're trying to keep a sense of humor about this to keep me from getting angry.

Harrelson

Then more experts arrived. There was the toxicologist, environmental specialist, solid waste specialist, and vermin specialist. For several days, they picked through the trash.

Finally, the health commissioner had an announcement. "We did not find any conditions presenting a health hazard, and there were no distinctive odors." Even the rodent specialist said that there were no rodents.

Still, the barge had a court order not to unload its garbage. Police boats were assigned the unwanted duty of babysitting it.

New York Harbor Police

It's a pain in the neck.

Duffy St. Pierre

As the barge bobbed in the water, waiting for a place to dump its decaying trash, word spread of its long journey. People *wanted* to see the trash! Tourists got "a kick out of seeing it."

Phil Donahue

A popular talk show host of the 1980s leaped at the opportunity to do something dramatic. He climbed aboard the barge and reported atop the trash, microphone in hand. He was then photographed jumping into the garbage below.

Finally, a judge ordered that the barge's restraining order be lifted.

State Supreme Court Justice

Time is of the essence. Therefore I urge the city, state, and all concerned get on the ball.

Unfortunately, the Islip town supervisor who had offered to take the garbage changed his mind. Now he offered to take only half of the 3,186 tons. "Haul it to Gracie Mansion," he said sarcastically.

Gracie Mansion, home of the New York City mayor

Meanwhile, the *Break of Dawn* was told that it could tow the barge to New Jersey, next to the George Washington Bridge. Only . . .

New Jersey didn't want it anywhere near its state either! A New Jersey senator sailed out to the barge. "It stinks," he remarked.

Meanwhile, Greenpeace activists left a message.

By now the barge had been floating in the ocean for five months and traveled more than six thousand miles. Finally, a judge ruled that the trash should be burned.

Men in white suits and white masks used pitchforks to pick through the piles. Then it was burned in big ovens. "Good riddance," remarked the sanitation commissioner.

And that is what happened to the then 3,186 tons of trash that was now 400 tons of ash.

Come Aboard the *Break of Dawn*

Captain Duffy St. Pierre thought that his trip would be over in a week. Boy was he wrong! People wondered how the crew survived all those months wandering aimlessly at sea. "We have TV, radio, books," St. Pierre said. "We have contact with the shore. There's checkers and we play a little chess once in a while." The *Washington Post* wrote, "The ship freezer is well stocked with chicken, steak and hamburgers. Several weeks' supply of breakfast cereal is neatly stacked in the kitchen, opposite a beaming portrait of President Reagan."

Still, "It's been pretty boring," St. Pierre remarked and admitted "the best way to kill time is sleeping." The captain was also eager to take calls and visits from reporters because, as he confided, "we need the company." To further kill time, the crew looked over the plentiful news articles written about them. The captain complained to a visitor that a photo of him in a news article "makes me look as if I have only one eye." The visitor remarked, "You should wear a patch. You would look like a pirate. The garbage pirate."

The ship's fly infestation was problematic. St. Pierre had a solution. "We put poison down; they take one bite of the stuff and they burst into fire." Although there were many flies, thanks to the ocean and the elements, the barge's contents became odorless. "The last four days coming here we

Workers inspecting garbage on barge

had twenty-foot seas bust over the barge and the salt has eaten anything that was rotten in there. We have been walking around and jumping in the stuff. We have no fear of it."

Despite all of the drama surrounding the barge, St. Pierre remained steadfast in his opinion of Lowell Harrelson, calling him "the nicest gentleman you've ever met in your life." He said that he put "his heart and soul" into the garbage project.

After many months at sea, the *Break of Dawn* was relieved of its duty. Another boat was put in charge of babysitting the barge in New York City. The blue-and-white tug tooted twice as it arrived back at its home of Louisiana to cheers and the pops of champagne corks. The three-man crew—David Soto, Desmond Bowman, and

Task force member inspecting pile of garbage on barge

Elsbert Bowden—and their captain were greeted by family. Duffy St. Pierre's wife, Esther, recalled meeting her husband in New York. She said "It was wonderful, the Statue of Liberty in front of us and we were watching the garbage barge. Only in America." When asked if St. Pierre would tow the barge again, he said, "Why not?" His wife wasn't so sure.

The *Break of Dawn* at sea

Garbage Barge Facts

- According to business associates, Harrelson paid $6,000 a day to rent the barge, quickly erasing an estimated initial profit of $60,000. Much money was lost.
- Some nicknames for the barge included: "the gar-barge," "the barge to nowhere," "the Flying Dutchman of Trash," and "the floating hot potato."
- Harrelson said, "Everybody likes a good joke and this [the garbage barge] has become a big joke. But if we can ever prove a real good use for garbage—such as the production of methane gas—then there won't be a garbage problem." It seems that Harrelson

was ahead of his time, as now many states and countries turn garbage into energy.
- Novelty gifts were made from the barge's garbage. The New York City Department of Sanitation had saved a one-and-a-half-ton bale "crickets and all." A mail order company sold small packets of the trash for ten dollars. New York City got 50 percent of the profits. "It's designer garbage. We sent some to Tiffany's," said the chairman for the mail order company. The trash came coated in plastic with a letter of authenticity.
- After Duffy St. Pierre hit dry land, he sold T-shirts for ten dollars

Garbage Barge Facts Continued

- each. They read TOUR THE SEAS WITH CAPT. DUFFY, GARBAGE BARGE CRUISE LINES. According to one source, he made $100,000 from his venture.
- The 1987 barge was linked to the mob. Five companies that helped finance its failed trip were affiliated with organized crime. It was suspected that the mob was attempting to control the shipping of garbage from Long Island, though nothing illegal was done by attempting to ship the garbage to North Carolina.
- Most people don't know that a reporter named Susan Brozek Scott was the reporter who broke the story on a local North Carolina news channel. "It looked like a football field full of garbage," she later recalled. "When you're a reporter for a while you get that feeling in your stomach, like there could be a real story here." Boy was she right! Susan got word of the story on April Fools' Day. "I really thought he [the tipster] was pulling my leg at first."

Recycling Facts

- Recycling rose sharply after the garbage barge fiasco. The visuals of 3,186 tons of trash floating in the ocean were too powerful to ignore.
- Although we recycle far more than we did in 1987, we also create much more garbage (our population has also increased). According to the EPA, in 1985 we created 166 million tons of waste. In 2014, our waste creation rose to 258 million tons! Another study by the EREF suggests that we have created far more, stating that we created 340 million tons in 2014. Also according to the EPA, of the 258 million tons created in 2014, 136 million tons were sent to the landfill, 33 million tons were burned and turned into energy, 23 million tons were composted, and 66 million tons were recycled. Almost half of the materials recycled consisted of paper and paper board. Yard trimmings made up almost a quarter. Glass and plastics were both a little over 3 percent. Almost 30 percent of the trash generated were containers and packaging materials.
- The EPA also states that in 1985 we recycled 16 million tons of trash. In 2014 we recycled 66 million tons. That's quite a difference!
- Recycling paper uses less energy than making paper from a tree. Glass can be recycled over and over again while plastic cannot.
- Batteries have the highest recycling rate at 99 percent.

Garbage Facts

- There are thousands of active landfills in the United States.
- Scientists estimate that it will take up to one thousand years to break down a plastic bottle in a landfill.
- Plastic bottles are made from fossil fuels, which are not renewable resources.
- Plastic bottles can only be recycled once or twice while metal and glass can be recycled indefinitely. Paper can be recycled a handful of times.
- The trash business is a billion dollar industry. Some states make considerable money taking other states' trash.
- Food in a landfill can become mummified. In 1992 an archaeologist examined a landfill and found forty-year-old hot dogs, well-preserved guacamole, and heads of lettuce that looked as good as the day they were thrown out.
- A woman in Missouri had thrown out a $400,000 wedding ring in the trash! She never thought she'd find it, but after only an hour and a half search, she found it among tons of rotting garbage.
- Being a sanitation worker is one of the most dangerous jobs in the United States.

Ocean Garbage Facts

- In 1992, a shipping container fell overboard on its way to the United States from Hong Kong. It was filled with little yellow plastic duckies—28,000, to be exact! These rubber ducks have shown up on shores around the world, illustrating how far garbage in the ocean can travel.
- Author Donovan Hohn said, "I've also heard of crates full of cigarettes going overboard, which of course end up having their butts ingested by marine animals. In fact, one of the endnotes in my book lists the contents of a dead whale's belly: it was full of trash. Plastic pollution is a real problem."
- In the ocean, plastics do not disintegrate, but instead break up into tinier and tinier pieces. The amount of micro plastics in the ocean is concerning. Marine life mistake this plastic for food, which can be deadly.

The best way to save the environment is to reuse! Below are some projects others have done with items that would normally go to the landfill. Try your own!

Rocket made out of a shipping tube

Office building made out of shipping containers in Providence, Rhode Island

Pencil holders made out of soup cans

Car painted on recycled cardboard

Construction cone man greeting drivers on Interstate 95

Christmas tree decorated with found objects

Flower planters made from plastic bottles

Photo © Thinkstock

Select Bibliography

Akron (OH) Beacon Journal. "Garbage Barge at Sea—Somewhere." April 19, 1987.

Albuquerque Journal. "EPA Inspects Exiled Barge for Toxins." May 5, 1987.

Arizona Republic. "Garbage Ship Given Clean Bill of Health to Return NY Trash." May 20, 1987.

———. "NY Garbage Rotting on Barge after Third State Denies Entry." April 18, 1987.

Asbury Park (NJ) Press. "Fate Remains Uncertain for Garbage Barge." May 18, 1987.

———. "Judge Will Decide Garbage Barge Fate." May 26, 1987.

———. "Senator Wages Battle to Keep Garbage Barge Away from N.J." June 3, 1987.

———. "Tourists Interested in Garbage Barge." June 22, 1987.

Asheville (NC) Citizen-Times. "Barge Chugs North." May 10, 1987.

Bloomington (IL) Pantagraph. "Dock Plans Delayed as Barge Tested." May 19, 1987.

Decatur (IL) Herald and Review. "Garbage Barge Goes Up in Smoke (Finally)." September 2, 1987.

Des Moines Register. "Burn Garbage Barge's Cargo Says Panel, but Borough Says No." July 11, 1987.

Detroit Free Press. "Bahamas Says No; Barge Still Seeking Site for N.Y. Trash." May 8, 1987.

Dobbs, Michael. "On Garbage Boat Pride Sustains." *Washington Post.* May 10, 1987.

Indianapolis Star. "Louisiana Officials Guard Barge Carrying 3,000 Tons of Garbage." April 18, 1987.

Galveston (TX) Daily News. "Bahamas Spurns Garbage Barge." May 8, 1987.

———. "Barge off Brooklyn Coast; Restraining Order OK'd." May 18, 1987.

———. "Floating Garbage Somewhere in Gulf." April 19, 1987.

———. "Garbage Barge Can Come Home." May 13, 1987.

———. "Garbage Barge Disposal Plan OK'd." August 11, 1987.

———. "Mexico Turns Back U.S Garbage Barge." April 26, 1987.

Gearty, Robert. "Gar-barge in a Stall." *New York Daily News.* May 18, 1987.

Goldman, John J. "Garbage Barge Drawing N.Y. Tourists Like Flies." *Los Angeles Times.* May 19, 1987.

Gutis, Philip S. "The End Begins for the Trash No One Wanted." *New York Times.* September 2, 1987.

———. "For Alabamian, L.I.'s Garbage Is Dream Gone Bad." *New York Times.* May 6, 1987.

———. "For Trash Barge Crew, Empty Days and Flies." *New York Times.* May 4, 1987.

———. "Judge Lifts Ban in Garbage Case but City Doesn't." *New York Times.* May 29, 1987.

———. "Trash Barge to End Trip in Brooklyn." *New York Times.* July 11, 1987.

Hazleton (PA) Standard-Speaker. "Garbage Boat Skipper Uses Claim to Fame." August 19, 1987.

Hunter, Mary Jane. "Garbage Barge Monument to Environmental Misdeeds." *Florida Today.* May 11, 1987.

Kerrville (TX) Daily Times. "Trash Barge Encounters Legal Block." May 18, 1987.

Los Angeles Times. "For Sale: Well-Traveled Trash (Barge Not Included)." November 8, 1987.

———. "Garbage Out, Garbage In, Islip Decides." May 13, 1987.

McFadden, Robert D. "Garbage Barge Returns in Search of a Dump." *New York Times.* May 18, 1987.

McShane, Larry. "Garbage Barge Sits in N.Y. Harbor Awaiting Decision." *Journal News* (White Plains, NY). May 24, 1987.

Morning News (Wilmington, DE). "Garbage Barge Sits off N.Y. Harbor." May 18, 1987.

Neumeister, Lawrence. "Nation's Best-Known Garbage Heap Comes to Fiery Finish." *Hazleton (PA) Standard-Speaker.* September 2, 1987.

———. "N.Y. Town Says It'll Take Only Half of Barge's Garbage." *News Journal* (Wilmington, DE). June 2, 1987.

News Journal (Wilmington, DE). "Garbage Barge Hits Legal Snag." May 18, 1987.

Palm Beach (FL) Post. "2 New York State Sites Willing to Take Garbage." May 6, 1987.

———. "Federal Health Agents Probe Garbage Barge for Hazards." May 6, 1987.

———. "Garbage Barge Ends 155-Day Saga at Brooklyn Dock." August 25, 1987.

———. "Union Workers Trash Plan for Dumping Garbage Barge." July 13, 1987.

Paris (TX) News. "Garbage Barge Hits Legal Blockade." May 18, 1987.

———. "Garbage Barge Waits and Waits." May 26, 1987.

Reno (NV) Gazette-Journal. "Homeless Garbage Barge in New York Harbor." May 18, 1987.

Republic (Columbus, IN). "Odyssey Is Over." August 25, 1987.

Salina (KS) Journal. "Garbage Barge Junk Offered as Designer Gift." November 7, 1987.

Shabecoff, Philip. "With No Room at Dump, U.S. Faces a Garbage Crisis." *New York Times.* June 29, 1987.

St. Louis Post-Dispatch. "Unwanted Trash Barge Checked." May 5, 1987.

Tierney, John. "The Reign of Recycling." *New York Times.* October 3, 2015.

Other Resources

Action Speaks!. "1987 The Roaming Mobro Garbage Barge." Recorded at ASA220 on October 27, 2010, in Providence, RI, by Marc Levitt. http://actionspeaksradio.org/category/radio-show/page/5/.

Conover, Jr., John E. "The Garbage Barge." http://www.jconoverjr.com/g-barge.htm.

NBC Nightly News. "The Barge." YouTube video, 2:42, from news program televised by NBC in 1987. Posted by "KENNETH, WHAT IS THE FREQUENCY!?," December 6, 2015. https://www.youtube.com/watch?v=Dz86tLVXaI8.

Retro Report. *New York Times* video. "Voyage of the *Mobro 4000.*" May 21, 2013. https://www.nytimes.com/video/booming/100000002206073/voyage-of-the-mobro-4000html?action=click&contentCollection=booming&module=lede&region=caption&pgtype=article.

United States Environmental Protection Agency. "Advancing Sustainable Materials Management 2014 Fact Sheet." November 2016.

For a complete bibliography and further information, please go to meghan-mccarthy.com/allthattrash.html.

*To all the hardworking men and women
who collect our garbage every day.*

SIMON & SCHUSTER BOOKS FOR YOUNG READERS

An imprint of Simon & Schuster Children's Publishing Division

1230 Avenue of the Americas, New York, New York 10020

Text, illustrations, and all photos not otherwise noted copyright © 2018 by Meghan McCarthy

Photo of the *Break of Dawn* at sea used by permission. From *Newsday*, March 23, 1997 © 1997

Newsday. All rights reserved. Used by permission and protected by the Copyright Laws of the

United States. The printing, copying, redistribution, or retransmission of this

Content without express written permission is prohibited.

All rights reserved, including the right of reproduction in whole or in part in any form.

SIMON & SCHUSTER BOOKS FOR YOUNG READERS is a trademark of Simon & Schuster, Inc.

For information about special discounts for bulk purchases, please contact Simon & Schuster Special

Sales at 1-866-506-1949 or business@simonandschuster.com.

The Simon & Schuster Speakers Bureau can bring authors to your live event. For more information

or to book an event, contact the Simon & Schuster Speakers Bureau at 1-866-248-3049 or visit our

website at www.simonspeakers.com.

Book design by Chloë Foglia

The text for this book was set in Haboro.

The illustrations for this book were rendered in acrylic paint.

Manufactured in China

1217 SCP

First Edition

2 4 6 8 10 9 7 5 3 1

Library of Congress Cataloging-in-Publication Data

Names: McCarthy, Meghan, author.

Title: All that trash / Meghan McCarthy.

Description: First edition. | New York : Simon & Schuster Books for Young Readers, [2018] | "A Paula Wiseman Book."

Identifiers: LCCN 2017015054| ISBN 9781481477529 (hardcover) | ISBN 9781481477536 (eBook)

Subjects: LCSH: Barges–United States–Juvenile literature. | Refuse and refuse disposal–United States–Juvenile literature. | Mobro 4000

(Barge)–Juvenile literature. | Break of Dawn (Tugboat)–Juvenile literature. | Islip (N.Y.)–History–20th century–Juvenile literature. | Voyages and

travels–Juvenile literature. | Sea stories–Miscellanea.

Classification: LCC TD792 .M36 2018 | DDC 386/.244–dc23

LC record available at https://lccn.loc.gov/2017015054